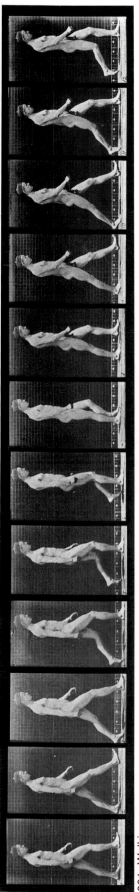

001 Walking.

002 Walking.

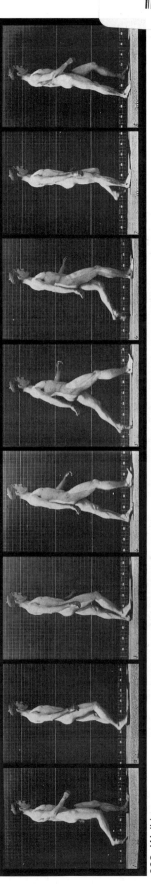

003 Walking.

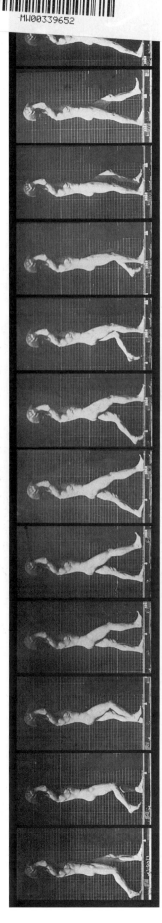

004 Walking and carrying a 75-lb. stone on head, hands raised.

1 MALES (NUDE)

Walking.

005

006

Running at full speed.

007

008

2 MALES (NUDE)

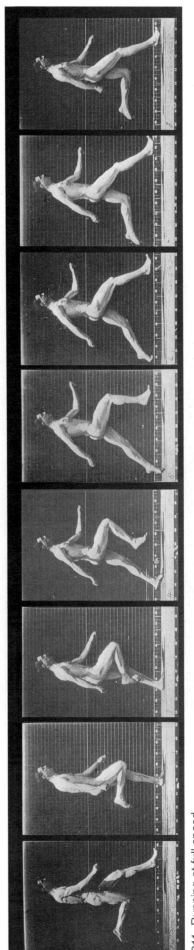

Running at full speed.

009

010

Running at full speed.

3 MALES (NUDE)

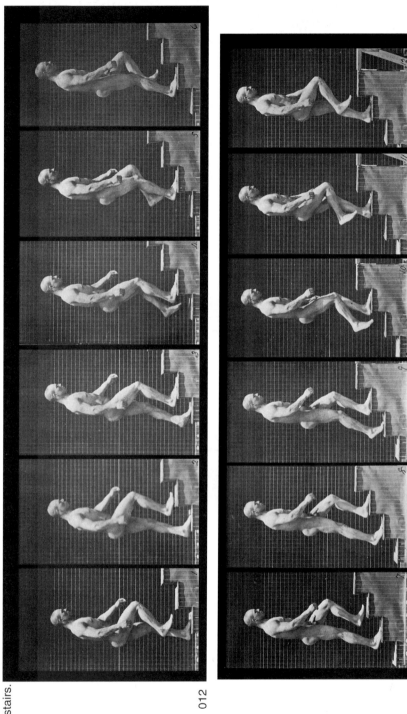

Ascending stairs.

012

013

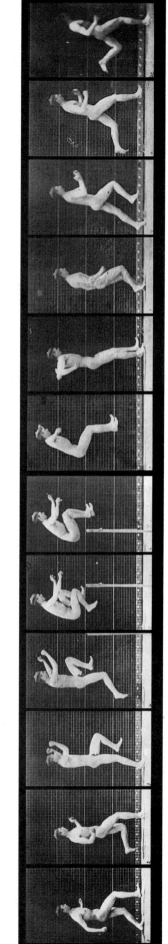

014 Jumping straight high jump.

4 MALES (NUDE)

Ascending a ladder.

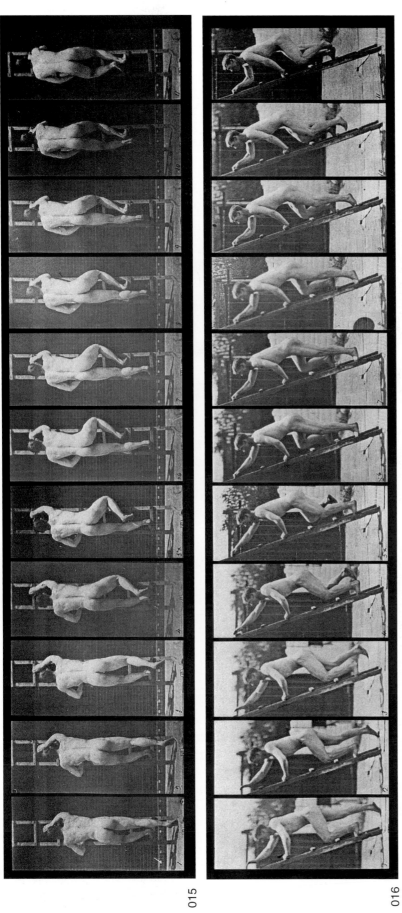

015

016

017 Jumping and pole vaulting.

5 MALES (NUDE)

018 Jumping and pole vaulting.

Descending an incline.

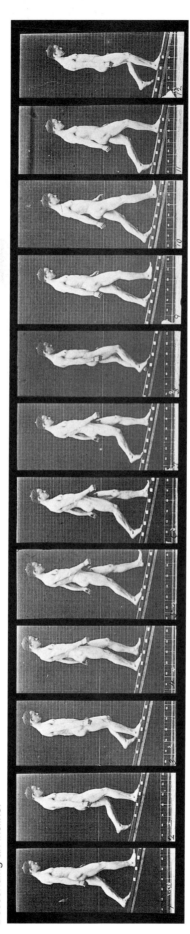

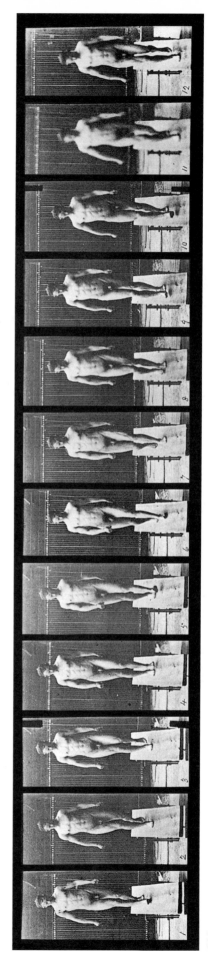

6 MALES (NUDE)

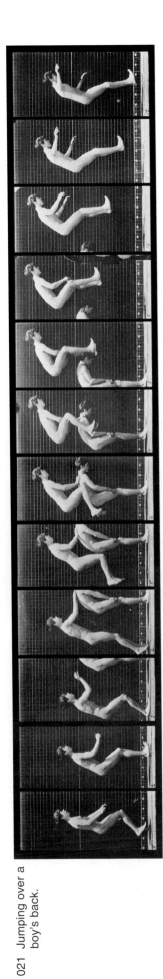

021 Jumping over a boy's back.

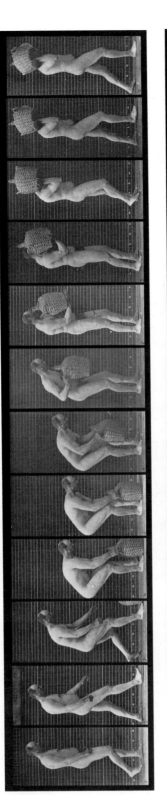

022 Stooping and lifting a full demijohn to shoulder.

Baseball, pitching.

023

024

Baseball, batting.

025

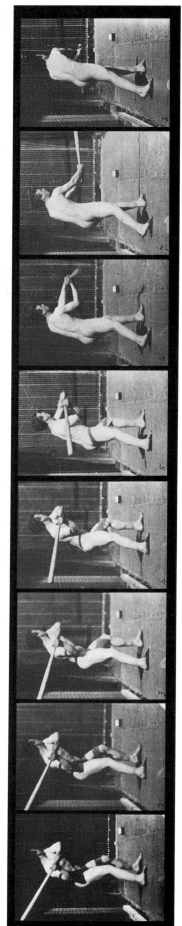

026

027 Baseball, running and picking up the ball.

8 MALES (NUDE)

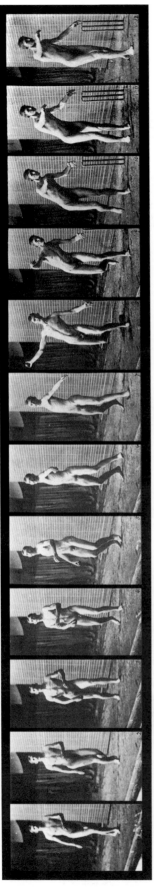

028 Cricket, round-arm bowling.

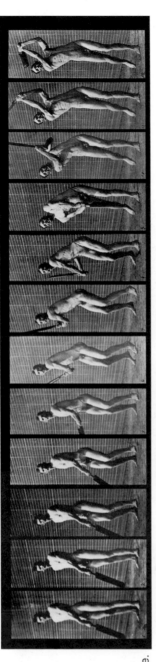

029 Cricket, batting and drive.

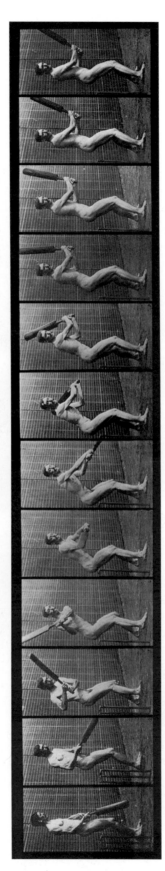

030 Cricket, batting and back cut.

031 Putting the shot.

Males (Nude) 9

Striking a blow with right hand.

032

033

034 First ballet action.

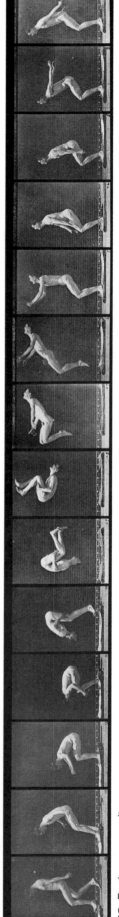

035 Back somersault.

10 MALES (NUDE)

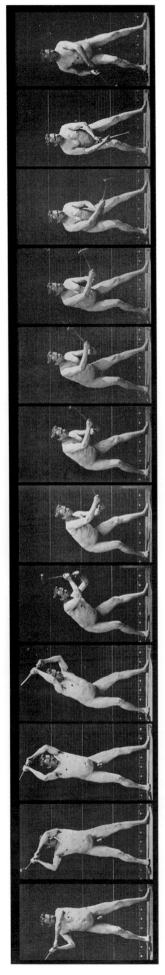

036 Blacksmith, hammering on anvil with two hands.

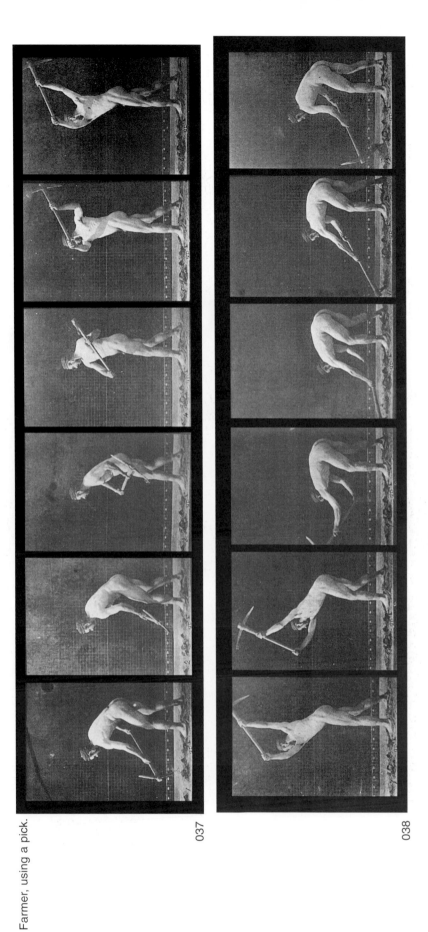

Farmer, using a pick.

037

038

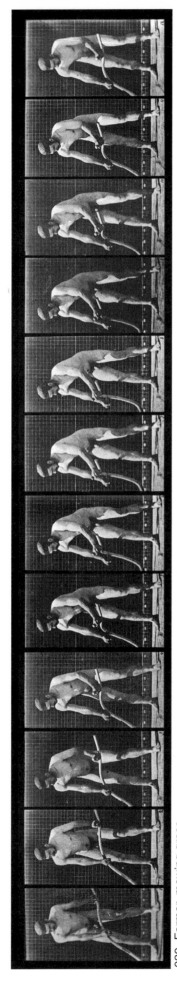

039 Farmer, mowing grass.

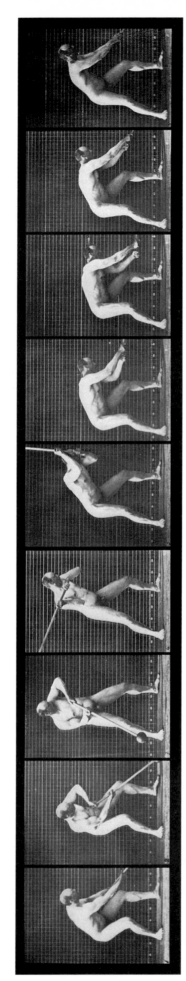

040 Pounding with a mallet.

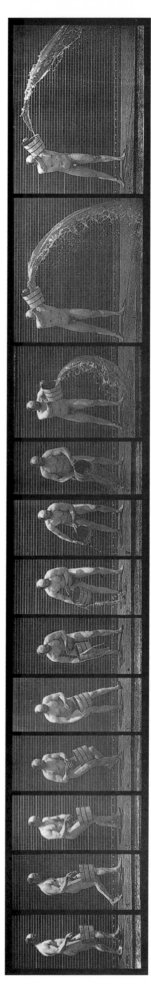

041 Emptying a bucket of water.

12 MALES (NUDE)

042 Ascending incline.

Using a pick.

043

044

13 Males (Nude)

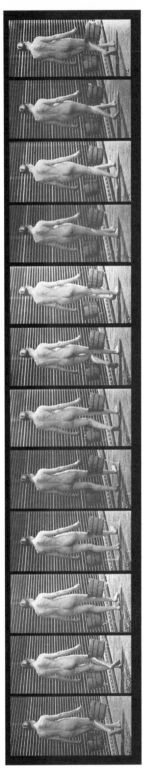

045 Walking and carrying a bucket of water in each hand.

046 Walking and carrying a 14-lb. basket on head, hands raised.

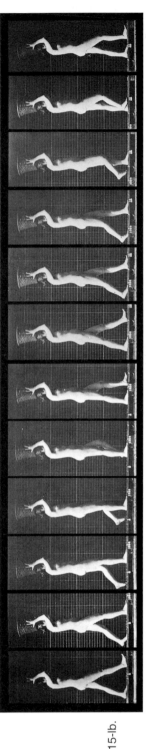

047 Walking and carrying a 15-lb. basket on head, hands raised.

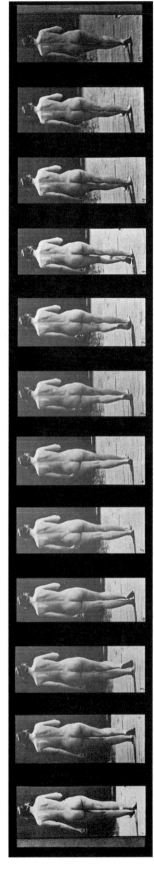

048 Walking, right hand at chin.

14 FEMALES (NUDE)

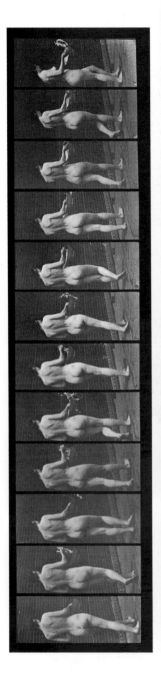

049 Walking, sprinkling water from a basin and turning around.

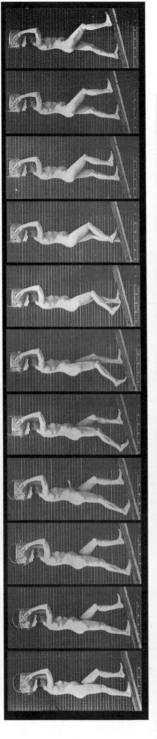

050 Ascending an incline with a 20-lb. basket on head.

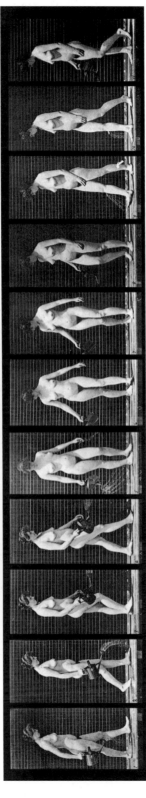

051 Walking, turning around and using a sprinkling pot.

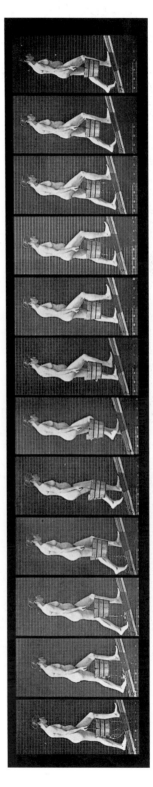

052 Ascending an incline with a bucket of water in each hand.

15 FEMALES (NUDE)

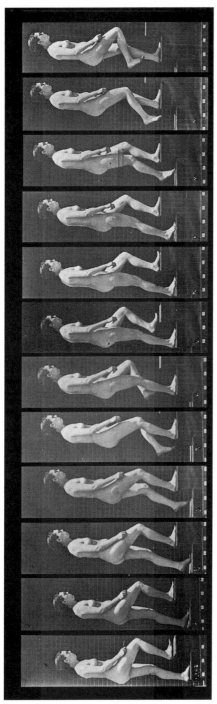

053 Ascending stairs.

Turning and ascending stairs.

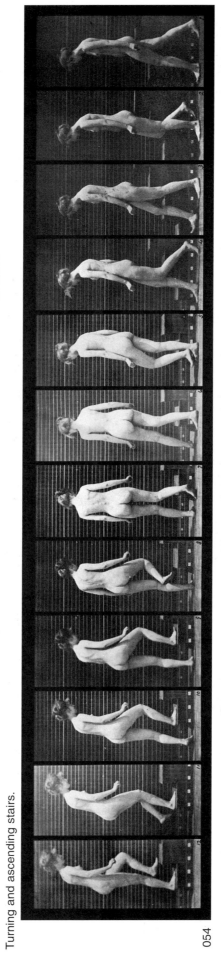

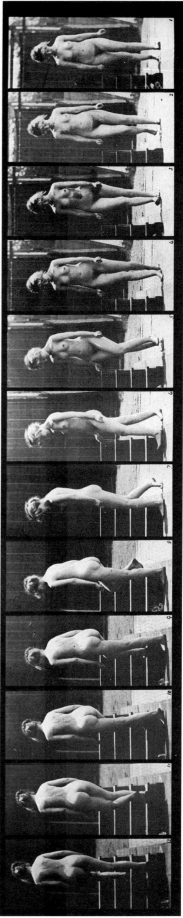

16 FEMALES (NUDE)

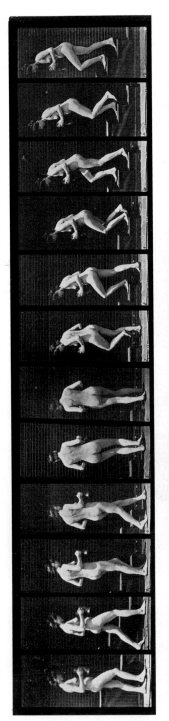

056 Turning and ascending stairs with a pitcher and goblet in hands.

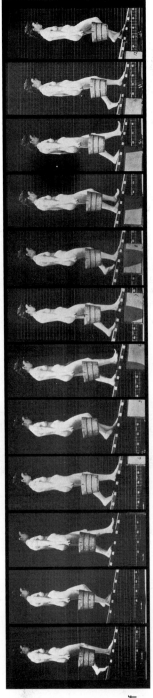

057 Descending an incline with a bucket of water in right hand.

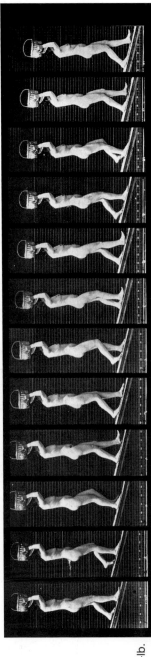

058 Descending an incline with a 20-lb. basket on head, hands raised.

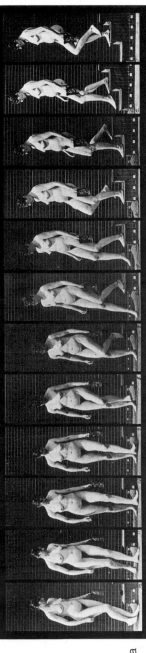

059 Descending stairs and turning with a pitcher in left hand.

17 FEMALES (NUDE)

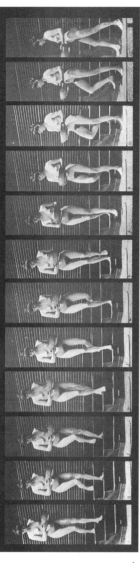

060 Descending stairs and turning with a basin in hands.

061 Jumping, running straight high jump.

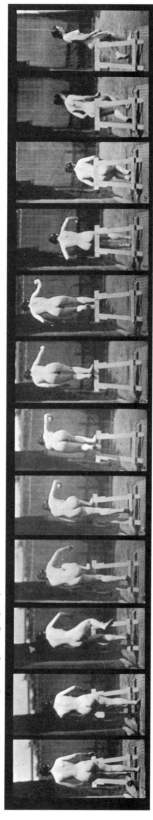

062 Stepping up on a trestle, jumping down and turning.

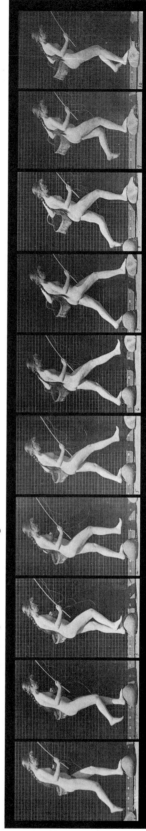

063 Crossing brook on stepping-stones with fishing pole and a basket.

18 FEMALES (NUDE)

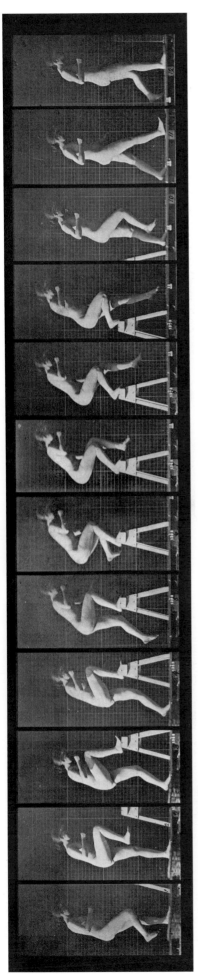

064 Stepping on and over a trestle.

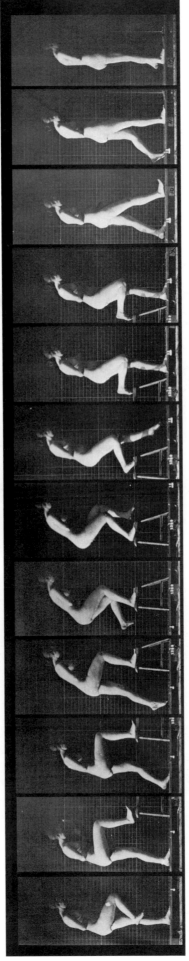

065 Stepping on and over a chair.

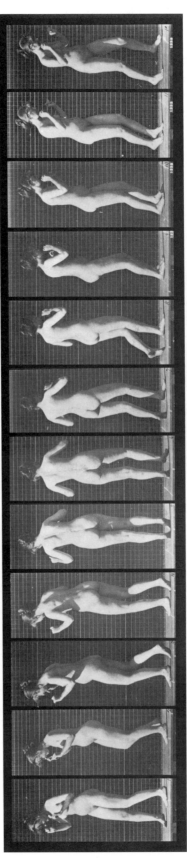

066 Dancing a waltz.

19 FEMALES (NUDE)

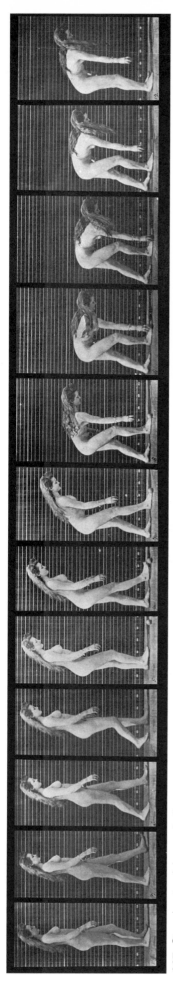

067 Stooping to pick up a ball.

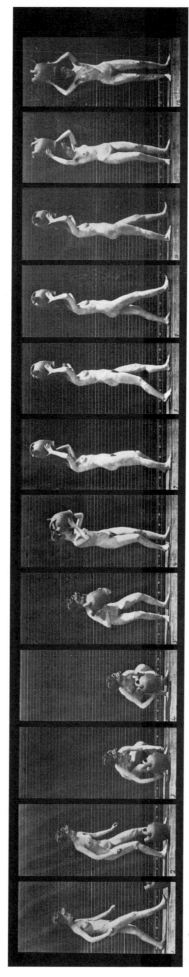

068 Stooping, lifting a water jar to head and turning.

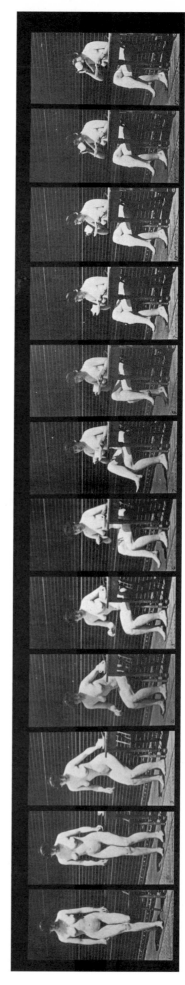

069 Sittiting on a chair, crossing legs and drinking from a teacup.

20 FEMALES (NUDE)

070 Sittiting down and placing feet on chair.

071 Kneeling on right knee and scrubbing the floor.

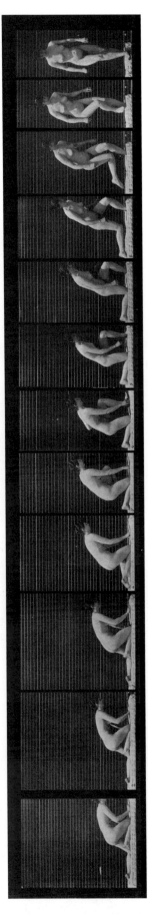

072 Arising from kneeling and turning.

073 Lying on the ground and reading.

21 FEMALES (NUDE)

Picking up a ball and throwing it.

074

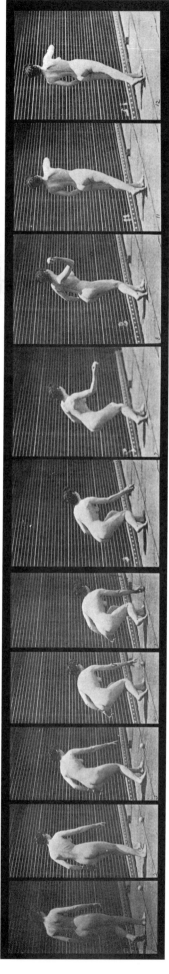

075

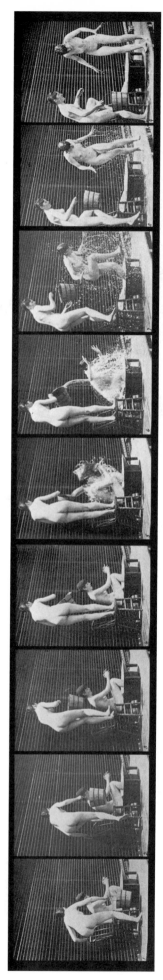

076 Woman pouring a bucket of water over another woman.

22 FEMALES (NUDE)

Woman pouring a bucket of water over another woman.

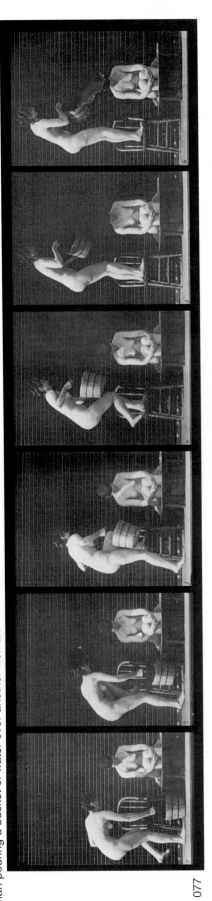

077

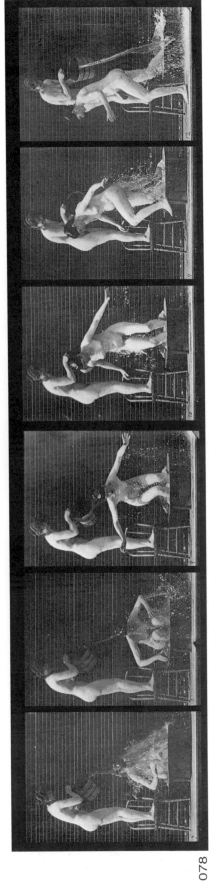

078

079 Lifting a towel while sitting and wiping feet.

23 FEMALES (NUDE)

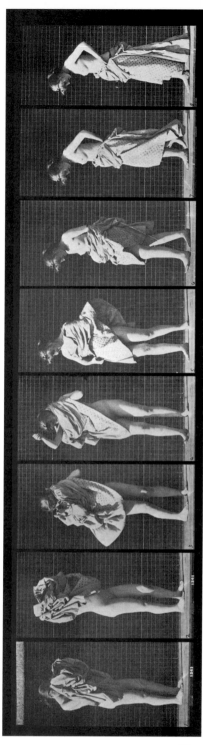

080 Toilet, putting on a dress and turning
     around.

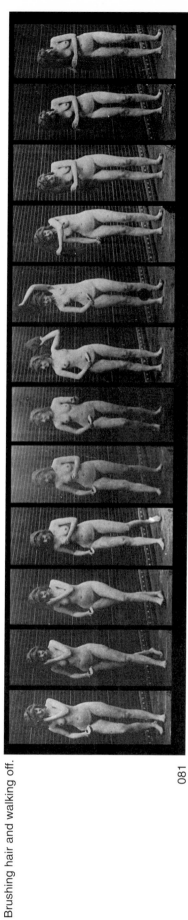

Brushing hair and walking off.

081

082

24 FEMALES (NUDE)

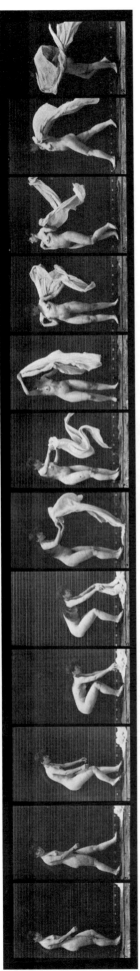

083 Toilet, stooping and throwing wrap around shoulders.

Taking off clothing.

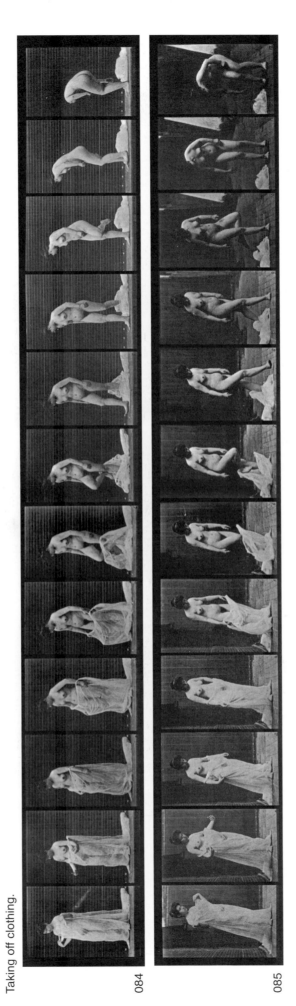

084

085

086 Wringing clothes.

25 Females (Nude)

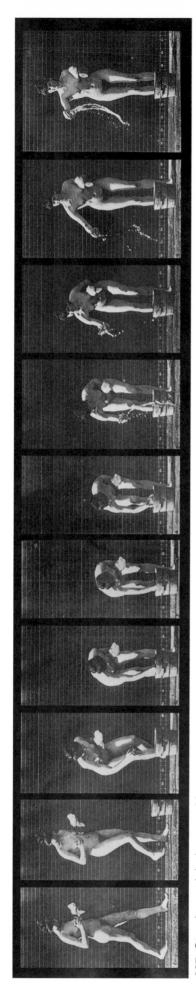

087 Stooping and rinsing a tumbler.

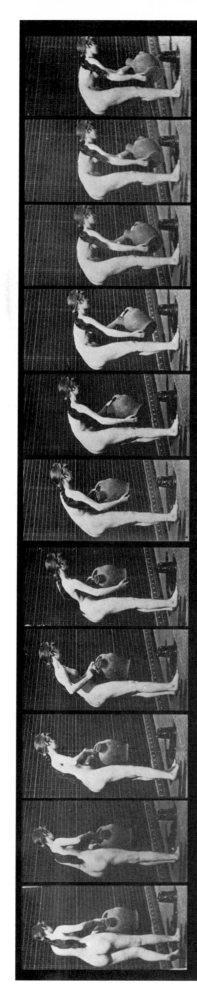

088 Filling a pitcher on the ground from a water jar.

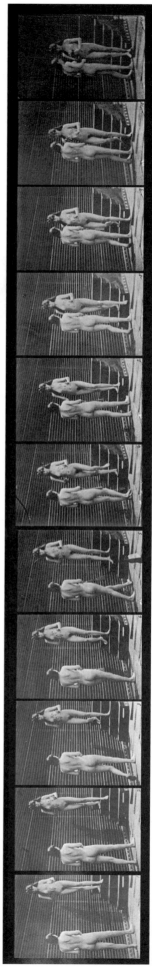

089 Woman descending stairs with a goblet meets another woman with a bouquet.

26 FEMALES (NUDE)

Miscellaneous phases of the toilet.

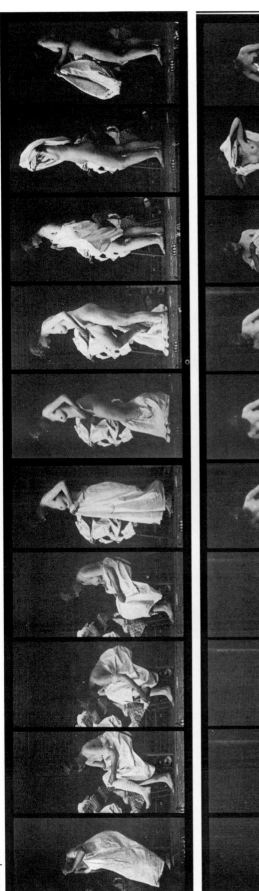

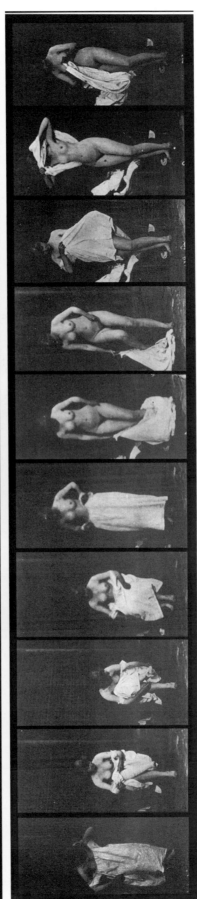

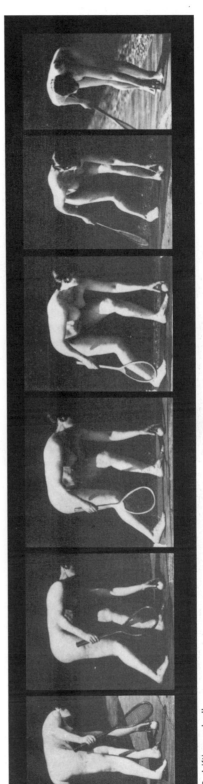

092 Lifting a ball.

27 FEMALES (NUDE)

093 Walking.

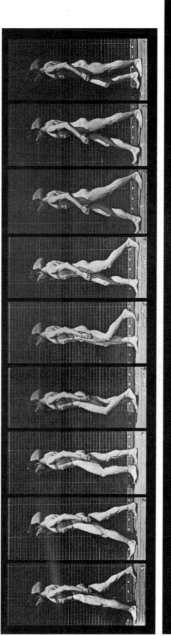

094 Walking, carrying a 75-lb. stone on right shoulder.

095 Jumping, running broad jump.

096 Jumping, running twist high jump.

28 Males (Pelvis Cloth)

Boxing, open hand.

097

098

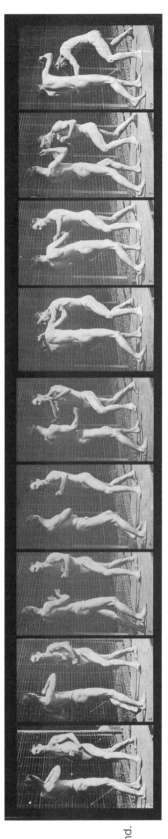

100 Boxing, open hand.

Fencing.

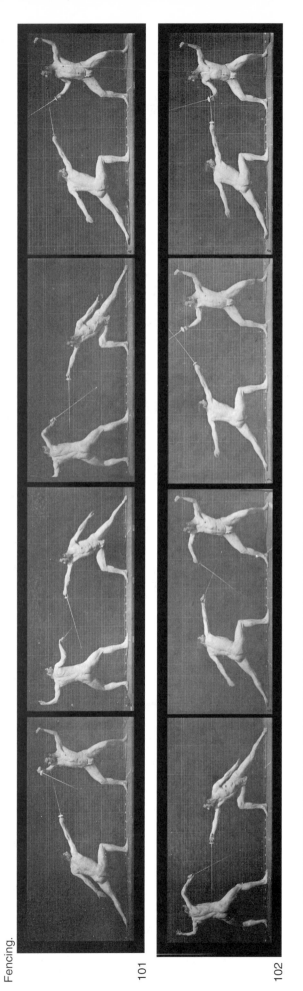

101

102

103 Fencing.

30 MALES (PELVIS CLOTH)

104 Kneeling, firing and rising.

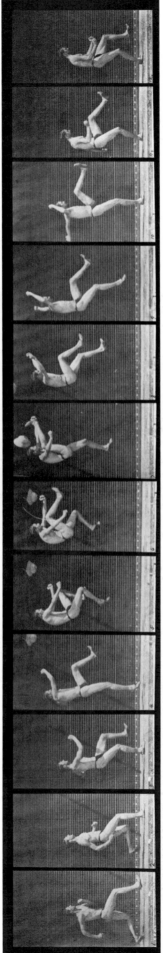

105 Running, hitch and kick.

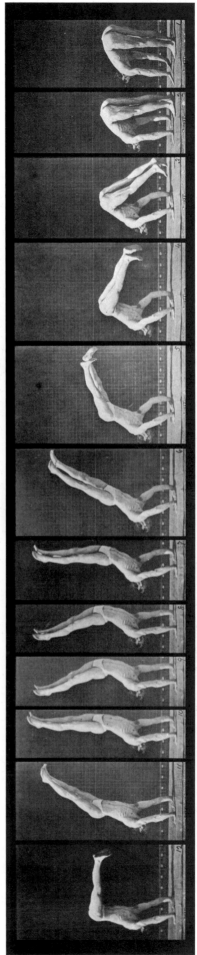

106 Acrobat, vertical "press up." (Note: This sequence is in reverse order as in the original book.)

31 MALES (PELVIS CLOTH)

Blacksmiths, hammering on anvil.

107

108

109

Walking, turning and stooping to lift train.

110

111

Stooping to lift train and turning.

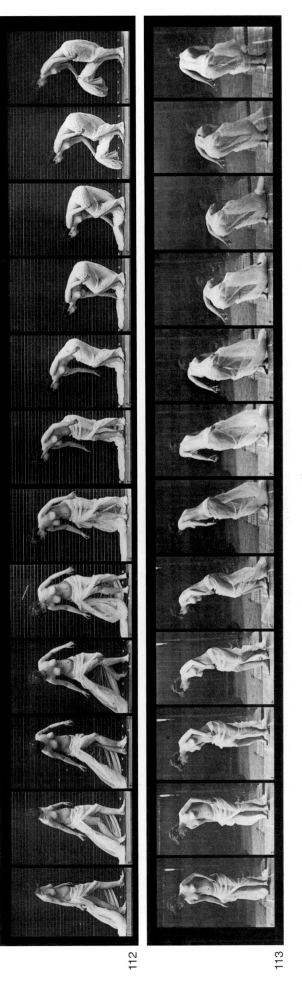

112

113

33 FEMALES (SEMI-NUDE) & CHILDREN

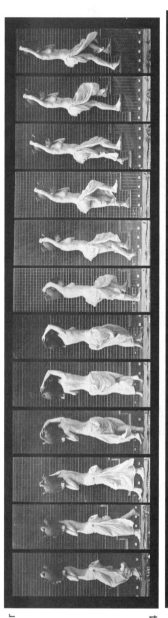

Turning and ascending stairs, a water jar on left shoulder.

114

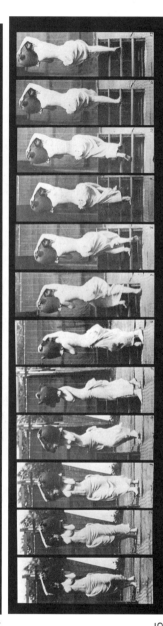

115

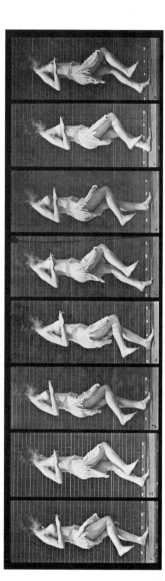

116 Hopping on left foot.

117 Miscellaneous phases of the toilet.

34 FEMALES (SEMI-NUDE) & CHILDREN

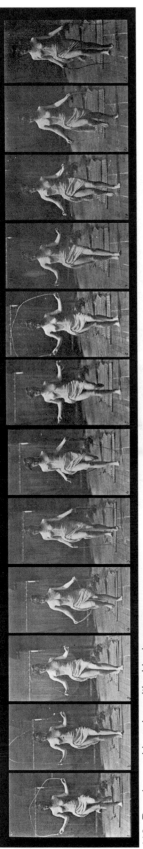

118 Running and jumping with skipping rope.

119 Sitting down on the ground.

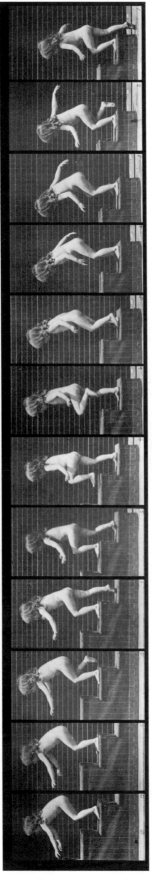

120 Child walking up stairs.

121 Child lifting a doll, turning and walking off.

35 FEMALES (SEMI-NUDE) & CHILDREN

Child bringing a bouquet to a woman.

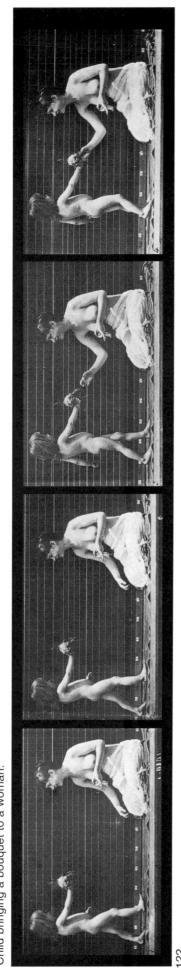

122

123

124

36 FEMALES (SEMI-NUDE) & CHILDREN

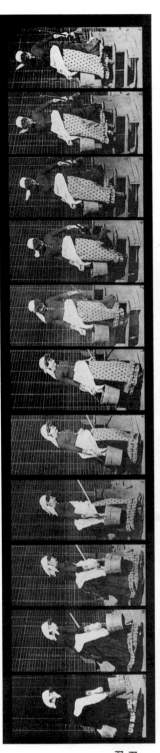

125 Descending stairs, turning and carrying a bucket of water and a broom.

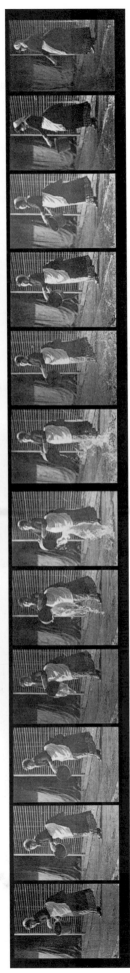

126 Emptying a bucket of water.

Sitting and flirting a fan.

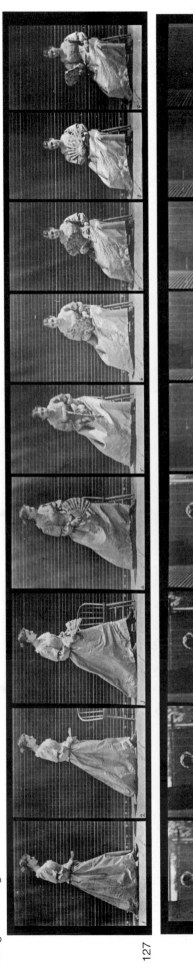

127

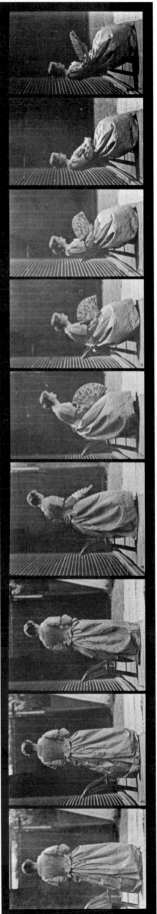

128

37 Males & Females (Draped)

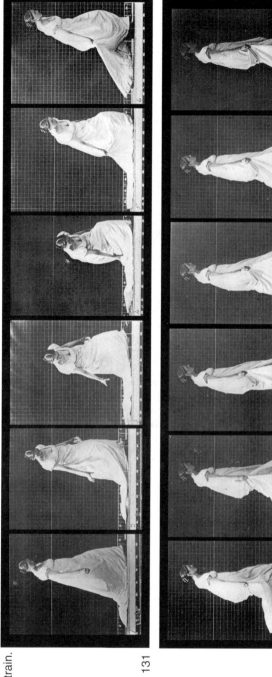

Turning and ascending stairs.

129

130

Stooping and lifting train.

131

132

Jumping over boy's back
(leapfrog).

133

134

135

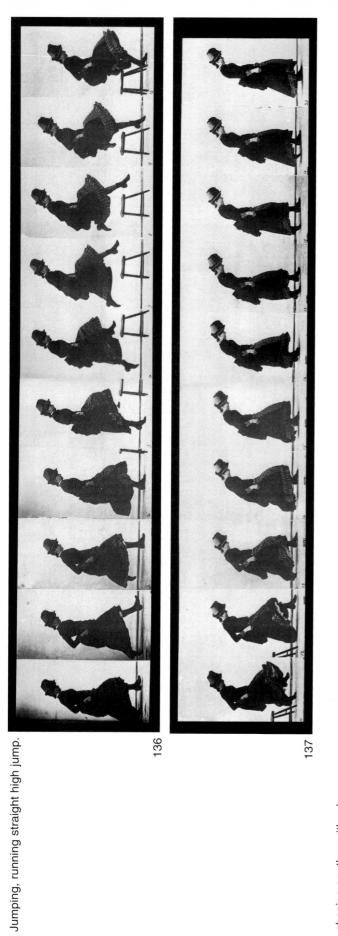

Jumping, running straight high jump.

136

137

Woman chasing another with a broom.

138

139

40 MALES & FEMALES (DRAPED)

Man and woman dancing a waltz.

140

141

Lawn tennis.

142

143

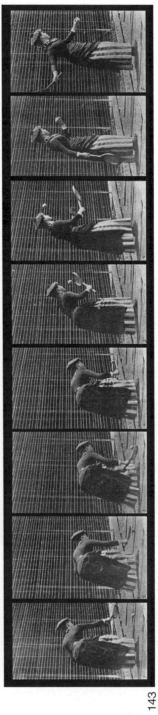

Lawn tennis.

144

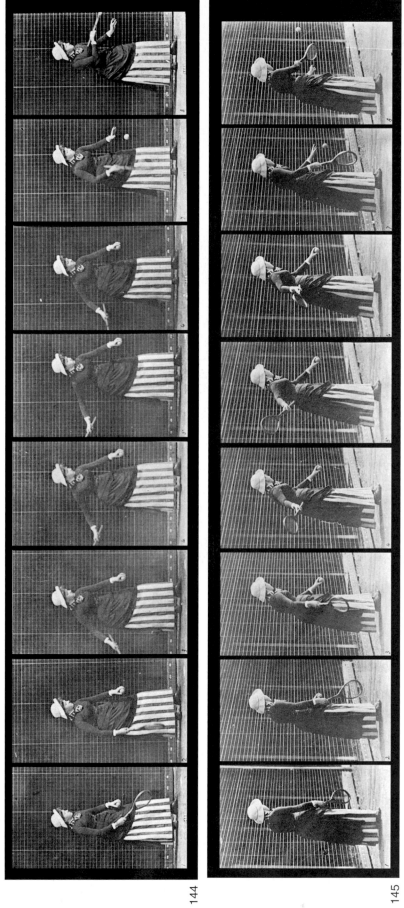

145

146 Lawn tennis.

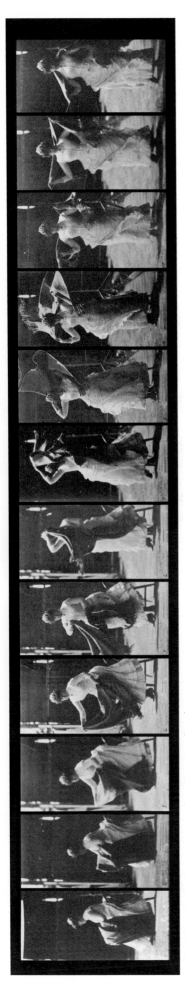

147 Toilet, rising from chair and putting on shawl.

Raking hay.

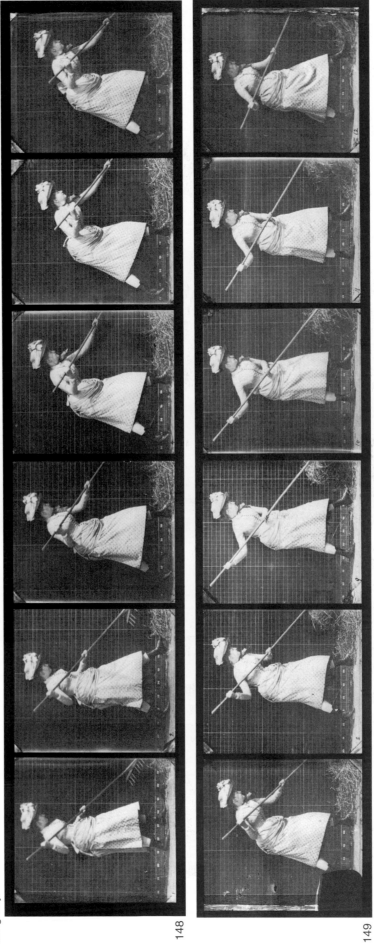

148

149

Walking and turning around rapidly with a satchel in one hand, a cane in the other.

150

151

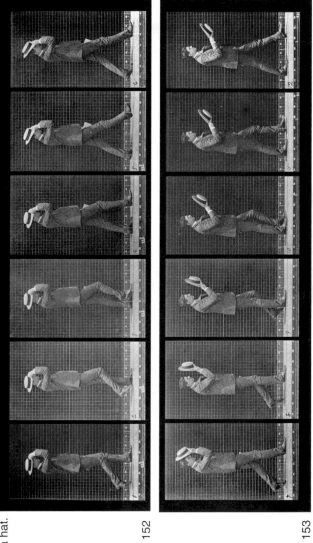

Walking and taking off a hat.

152

153

Miner, using a pick.

154

155

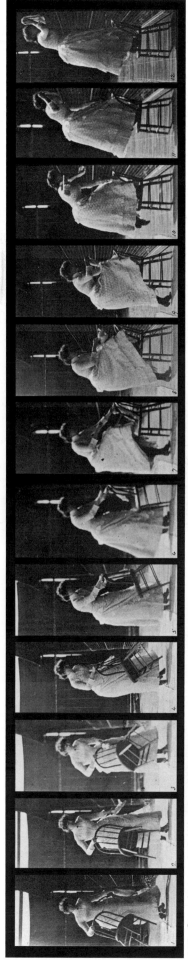

156 Stepping on a chair and reaching up.

45 MALES & FEMALES (DRAPED)

Sitting down, rising, etc.

157

158

Movement of the hand, beating time.

159

160

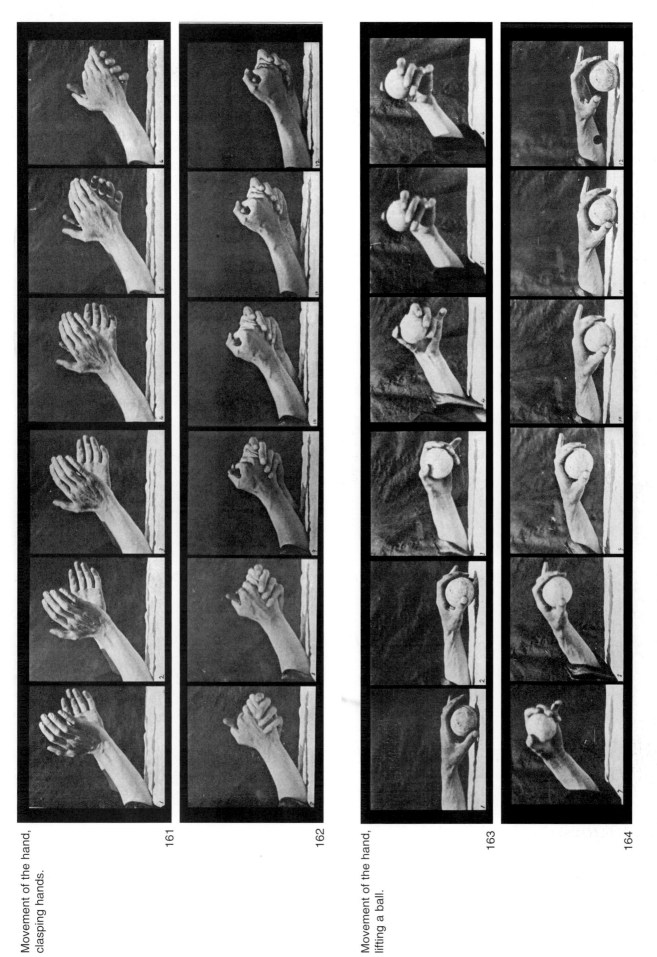

Movement of the hand,
clasping hands.

161

162

Movement of the hand,
lifting a ball.

163

164

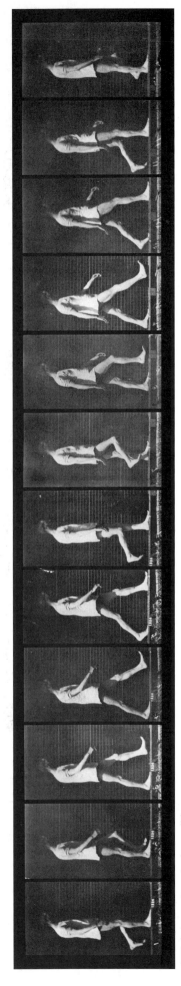

165 Locomotor ataxia, walking

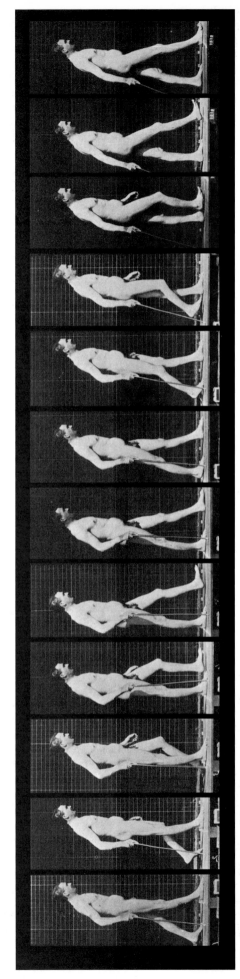

166 Partial paraplegia, walking with cane.